Towards A New Compass

poems by

Lorne Daniel

ISBN 0-920066-15-1   (paper)
ISBN 0-920066-16-x   (cloth)

Book design and cover by Neil Wagner.

Published Spring 1978 by

Thistledown Press
668 East Place
Saskatoon, Sask.

Acknowledgements:

Some of the poems have appeared or will appear in

     CANADA GOOSE

     THE CANADIAN FORUM

     NEBULA

     REPOSITORY

     WAVES

Several of the poems were heard on CBC radio's
"Anthology". Other poems appeared in the book,
STORM WARNING 2 (McClelland & Stewart). The poem,
"Bird" was published in Lorne Daniel's earlier
collection of poems, *THE HUNTING HAND*,
(Red Deer College Press, 1973).

CONTENTS

compass -- *1. an instrument*
for determining direction by means
of a needle pointing to the magnetic
north *2. an instrument*
for drawing and dividing circles;
also called 'dividers'
  3. range; extent;
boundary: "the compass of a voice"

THE WINSTON DICTIONARY OF CANADIAN ENGLISH

Winter

WINTER

Winter came in weeks ago:
the three days of snow
that we know won't go away for months
Remnants of insulation from Pat's cabin
near Rocky Mountain House
went into the ceiling
and weather tape around the doors
Storm windows came out
of the basement and garage
every second pane broken   In my study
poems were set aside
putty and knives and new glass brought in
Now   the old glass remains
scattered over old newspapers
in pieces and slivers
like a mine field: sharp pain
strikes my every step
towards poetry   I must be satisfied
with warmth while snow twists
around me   drifting into
cracks in the walls   empty spaces
I didn't have time to fill

The eaves leak: every warm day
leaves a path
of ice alongside the house   Eric fell
and scraped his head against the basement wall
yesterday   He will remember
not to walk on ice
I will watch the gash heal
and the scabs slowly clear
and will remember the mark
long after his face is baby smooth
again   I will remember the ice
next year and talk of fixing the eaves
The ice   the eaves   the house
the year: winter is memory
something always there
in the background
at the beginning and end of everything

The freeze-frame of winter:
snow stops cars and their tracks
slides off mountain sides   blocking passes
Ice air stiffens cable
stops cranes   cats   snaps steel blades
Streams stop
Steam and exhaust stand in the sky
Shovelling through winter   I stop
to catch my breath   knowing I won't be able
to forget   In daydreams of warm places
winter remains like a boundary: snow
surrounding the house
arctic and antarctic capping
the lands between   defining
their warmth
Winter came in weeks ago   and will remain
forever

BIRD

A bird sits
poised on a fencepost
a shivering tuft of feathers
with tentative probing wings
but adamant fixed feet

This winter it seems
too frosty to fly   insane to stay
    (it will only get colder)
and ultimately impossible to decide
    decision by default
    the natural outcome
For to fly a short way
and return to sit
would make neither
the flying nor the sitting
any healthier

So I sit

slowly being frozen lifeless

by the elements

yet not knowing if flight

would bring warmth

or a quicker death

WINTER AT THE BANFF SCHOOL

I have been here many days
waiting
expecting something to happen
watching
            : tons of rock
unnaturally on edge
stone seams standing in the air
at the angle of repose
            : the snow
piling wet and heavy onto ledges
and evergreen limbs
From the window in this dark winter
room I see
            : Sue
nine months pregnant
tomorrow   her long blue gown framed
in the window across the courtyard

13

                    : a deer

climbing the slope

from the river   uncertain

of this light that is not moonlight

Across the snow   Sue watches

the doe   I think

of Sue's child and my son

back home and the fawn that may be

waiting

up the mountain

I am searching

for the voice that will speak

for all of us

but the doe and Sue

are moving

slowly

        silently

                    away

from the moment

                    : the doe

steps into the swirls of snow

cautiously

but is suddenly gone

her tracks blown over

                    : Sue's room

across the way

is dark

I stare into snow

that falls steadily   piles heavy

heavier on stretching   bending limbs

waiting

WINTER NIGHT: STEPPING OUT

In my fur coat
I am animal
I am watched
as I lope across well-kept city lawns
I am the shaggy shadow
between houses

The lights from a passing car
are intense   possessed   mechanical
and I react instinctively
step sideways
pad silent under dark pines

The smell from nearby
stock yards   the blood off the killing floor
makes me stop
test the wind
before I move on

Suddenly I slip on the ice
underfoot
and expecting four feet
find I have only two
and cannot correct my fall

I hit the hard ground hard
I am human

Old Frames

New Growth

HERITAGE

I often stagger
upon the image
of great-grandfather
fishing off the Hebrides coast
swaying in his boat
I don't doubt that
his home was much
the same as mine:
jars
with tartan labels and
emptied scotch bottles
clinking together
relatives on the wavering floor

PICTURE OF A GENERATION

Cracks
like baked earth
in the corners of
cool sharp eyes and
around the dry mouth
Brown layers crusted
over and tanned
rained   frozen   melted
dried in
The seasons
bring nothing but
change:
the red blood of birth
sticks   a skin-tight reality
of pain and possibilities
on an old frame

OLD PHOTOGRAPH : NEW SETTLEMENT

Inside the brown frame

the print fades

into sepia tones

the faces lose distinction

But behind the bodies

the logs have settled

into each other

and above the heads

the sod is knitting together

growing green

GROWING

Year one   : we couldn't believe
the leaping green   not only
what we planted but
edible pigweed between the rows
and a green barbed fence
of Russian thistles around it all
          : I sat and watched
the tangle with a cold bottle
moistening my palm
          : you embroidered
a flowering thistle on my shirt
       /a stroke of genius/

Year two   : the dead awaited us
refused to be moved by spring
winds
          : we were late
clearing the old away
          : broccoli grew late
into fall   wouldn't stop even
when we chopped at it   denting knives
on the frozen stalks

23

Year three : a three foot by three foot
wooden planter on the four foot by twelve foot
balcony of a two-bedroom
apartment on the twenty-first
floor at the corner of 121st
and 104th   we were counting
the days   watching the life grow
in your belly
            : you had trouble
bending over to harvest the small crop
at summer's end
            : I wiped your brow
and watched as Eric was born

Year four   : gardening at the farm again
despite the three hour round trip
our best garden yet
            : Eric slept
most of the way there and back
            : I planted
the potatoes (they kept
fresh in the wellhouse most of the winter)
            : we all grew
stronger

Year five   : a back yard of
our own (rototilling ˙topsoil
to work yard
junk to haul away fences
to build)
              : Eric storms
about digging dirt throwing sand
falling in post holes eating green plums
from low branches
              : you are growing
a child inside
again
              : I am watching
a 16 gallon crock of rhubarb wine
fermenting in the basement
              : the wild vigor
of past gardens   is gone
but delicate herb/spices are doing well
some are perennials will grow again

next year   :

AFTER THE COUNTRY

(for Fred and Ruth)

I have slivers in my fingers

and the palms of my hands

The posts were rough

The wire was wild and sharp --

when my hold slackened

it sprung its ambush of stinging barbs

Dust blew up from the fields

swirled seeds and grit into my face

and falls back now   grey powder

from my hair

Even after the earth has been washed

from the surface

my cough brings up dark reminders

This spring has pulled

the moisture from the ground

aged it to dry grey

This spring has pulled

the sweat from me   my skin

cracking   flaking   dry

The slivers will not stay forever

cells working upwards

forcing wood hairs out

Other flaws may remain

slight scars on smooth surfaces

And the seeds of the country

blown into my gut --

will they leave or stick   stay

inside me   take root

start something new   growing....

SEASON OF LEAVING (SYLVAN LAKE, ALBERTA)

1.
The season to leave is spring
or possibly fall
Summer holds
as it held my forefathers:
green and tangling
growing back
back where I cut it down
and trimmed its wildness
last year
Winter white challenges
with its assault on activity
of all kinds; snow traps
quickly   quietly
Even now the white weight
hugs the barn
towards the ground

2.

In town the buildings are all squat

half-sized and humorous

All winter long the windows

and skin-happy swimmers

have been in hiding

behind boards   terrorized

by stark flat miles of wild ice

On the way   driving down to Sylvan

I can see shades of the Pacific

    dark   warm   and blue

rolling over white-profiled mountains

Soon the seasonal decay begins

again   snow turning brown

winter   an empire gone decadent

and soft

3.

I have stopped

in the past   stayed

to add new limbs of life

to old wood

(always wood) frames:

new timbers   squared and strong

forced under the old

nailed into place as saviours

of some sad structure

Lately   though   I've been remembering

long-necked beer bottles

dark and musky

cob-webbed to roughed-in window sills:

I wonder if the lines I build

will stand as long

4.

Years ago   David Thompson
axed his way through trees
near here   enroute to
Rocky Mountain House and beyond
Now the Government of Canada
calls in engineers with fine instrumentation
to keep the last
remains of the fort
from washing down
the North Saskatchewan River
Nature keeps doing that:
washing back
downstream
down east
these pretences of civilization

In spring   I find myself
running with the water

Life Dances

LIFE DANCE
(for Patricia)

your smile steps through
dew-drop dog-bark
backwoods dawns

your lion-heart catpaws
play and prance
sun mane dances

how gently life leaps
from your eyes
to my awakening

SALTLICK

naive sculptors
lick
rough block
round:
draw art
from necessity

FALLING AWAY

(i)

The overhang breaks clean

like stone

under sculptor's hand

falls sharply

drops god-like

into mortalizing splash:

mud amidst

water's soft seduction

(ii)

Before you

I lose concentration

feel myself breaking:

noble intentions

falling away

LIFE AT 25,000 FEET, 800 MPH

(for babe-in-arms)

You sleep well

Your mother smokes

carefully butting

the cigarette every quarter inch

It must be her last one

She is getting near the end

and touchdown is not soon

You clutch firmly

at scarred wrists

hands that fidget

with your deep sleep

There is only one

oxygen mask between you

and this woman who holds you

so helplessly hopeful

In case of emergency

you need not be awakened

THE RAMBLER

The petals are soft   rumpled
paler than the posters and roadsigns
but recognizable still
The thorns tangle and twist around
a Rambler grill   Strange
to see roadsign emblems growing
wild   Next I suppose it'll be a snake
in a CN configuration
then digging for old bottles I'll find
an ancient Shell
yellow on a red background with a neon glow
I bring myself to this prickly task --
liberating a Rambler grill
from rose bushes
I know how good the chrome would look
grinning down at me from the concrete wall
as I sit at my desk and stare
at an imaginary horizon

I push heroically into the bush

but quickly scramble back   deciding

symbolism isn't worth

scratches and swelling sting   and abandon

the grinning grill

The car's shell around the other side of the bushes

doesn't look too promising   lodged

in last spring's mud

and tangles of weed

But I'd be satisfied if I could bag a hubcap

or steering wheel   hell   I'd settle for an ashtray

sporting a swirling "R"

No such luck   The hulk has been stripped

many times over   for many different motives

no doubt   What's left

is all bumps and dents and bends

as if beaten about

by a crazed Bigfoot

I don't know what the hell I'm doing in this ditch
I never owned a goddammed Rambler
and probably never will
I resolve not to consider anymore the possibilities
of seeing "Rambler" written across my walls
and walk on   my heavy duty
hiking boots beginning to
drag in the dirt   I'm beginning to
think there's nothing of interest
in the ditch
when a blasted rose scratches up inside my pant leg
I jerk back in a kicking dance
and the whole bloody thing comes out
by its white roots   exposing
an old license plate:
Alberta /BR 4113/ Wild Rose Country

Towards

A New Compass

WIND FROM THE WEST

(for Fred)

As I drive down into Sylvan the sky to
the East is clear
but dust clouds over the West horizon
and whitecaps chop the darkening lake
In town gathering gusts are hidden
by clustered buildings as white-limbed folks
bend over fences and windows preparing
for the sun   I pick up groceries
and mail a letter to Peter in his quiet home
behind the wind in the Kootenays
wondering -- will he understand
my dark rushed lines?
I head home North then East
the wind carrying dust I cannot outrun
on this rough road   Rumbling down
off a rise I scare up black
birds that rise East
then swing back   tilt
into the wind   soar
above the dust

42

Back at the farm the guys are in the barn
sampling Fred's rhubarb wine
He has no recipe
but watches the fruit   sugar
and yeast   knowing from experience
when they need nutrient
a stir   or stabilizer
Fred steps outside to help Don
pad a sculpture to be shipped down East
Wind/dust applies a final sandpapering
to the cedar as they work
and Fred swings the piece around
letting the wind wrap
padding tightly around sculpted beams
Fred saw this wind coming
early in the day   maybe even before that
Last night   like many nights before   he
and I sat on the deck
after the sun had left
and talked long of the stars and moon and planets

Fred looked into the sparkling dark   watched
the movement   needed to know how
these things work   like he knows
flywheels and circular saws   He needs to know
the mechanics of weather   the way
the earth turns   "This way"
he demonstrates with his hands (a god
spinning a beach ball/planet)
Now as I throw darts up against the West wall
I note the curl of the feathers   and air currents
and the darts whisper home with authority
I open the door to challenge
Fred to a game and instead
am challenged   full face   by the wind
I turn sideways and my ears are filled
with sounds of terror screaming across fields
from the direction of town
Fred steps past me
and speaks only of the delightful jangle
he hears from an older sculpture
(tin chimes on wood)
as it creates art
with the wind from the West

DRYLAND COUNTRY   SOUTHERN ALBERTA

the dramatic cruelty of the wind
on defenceless bluffs and hillsides goes
unnoticed   its ugliness equalled only
by the unattended sandscapes and waterless
hollow runs themselves
                         unnoticed
like vietnamese slaying
vietnamese
              the wind's own
momentum tossing soil against
soil is its only real force
two hundred miles away   the mountains
recognize the sham for what
it is   but no wonder
these hills try to slip quietly
away with every passing
rain

TOWARDS THE PASS

The wind out of the Pass

reaches 60 mph

rocking and bucking travelers like me

mistaking us for settlers

heading west

into the wind's secret home

behind the mountains

Some of the snow has not retreated

fast enough

and is swept over

with dust   blackened by dark chinook gusts

that do not tolerate such challenges

The patches that remain

are hiding   dirty white

under the lip of cut-banks

like so many skulls

The car I drive

would give up at such sights

if left to its own

It is my right foot

stretched uncomfortably in front of me

that forces such confrontations

I decide this is no day for sacrifice

there have been enough of those

along the road

When I turn North

making my good intentions known

the wind is suddenly co-operative

curling around the foot of mountains

fanning South

and North

urging the car along from behind

like a border patrol

as we run parallel

to the Rockies

EAST TO WEST

We fly Time Air over Alberta

thinking we know the difference

between grains: rape

barley   wheat

There are bruises

bulges under the skin of the earth

Roads attempt to stitch it all together

reaching along the ribs of coulees

that test the wind   test the water

blowing   flowing east

Erosion is the only permanence

A variety of implements cut at the land

never satisfied with what it produces

while mud rivers run

and dirt clouds by

We fly against the grain

wash ourselves clean

as wind and water clear

BOUNDARIES

rumbling numb
over brash flat
expanses

until: swirling
sharp/silver/blue
waves into blank pools
of eyes

rolling
towards rising ridges
scraping
/shoulder against cliff/
dirt skin on stone bone

until: rock slabs stand
in assertive line
a cold slap

defining
time
distance
existence

HEADWIND

Thin arms and legs
a vanguard of reaction
lead
        opposition
force
        confrontation
The blinding march
into the headwind
shakes away
all but the essence
Wills collide
head-on
clap together
into storm
as challenger and challenged
meet
eye-to-eye

TOWARDS A NEW COMPASS

(i) CONFRONTATION

like a driven thing
wild beneath the dust
mad under whirls of gritty hair
I am thrown against things
my back straightened
by gusts
        and walls
I stand tall
like headlines on a newspaper
shocked up tight to brick

there is no hint of a breeze
           in this West wind
and I would have it no other way
I seek the face-to-face
yet lashes and brows
lack my eyes' drive
and sabotage sight

I fall back watching

the pawns of this wind war:

stiffly proud old trees

transplanted from more peaceful lands

snap and splinter

pliable saplings

their tops whipped towards the ground

at an early age

grow in an arc

while rooting desperately at soil

they seek civilization

eventually settle

for survival

(ii) PEACE TREATIES AND INTERNATIONAL TRADE

upstream: Erickson's concrete Queen
beached on the dusty coulee's crest
where the Old Man hasn't run
for centuries
          :   down on the river flat
Fort Whoop-Up
a model/toy from this perspective (small
figures on crushed brick
paths that lead in sad circles)

from here   half way up the bridge   I see
nothing but peace and quiet
the whiskey traders have retreated
shrunk back into the Southern sun (well
beyond the International Peace Park)
leaving a dry road
to Mormons and Mounties

        but once a week the road is drunk
with pickups
(sidetracking Fords   windbrave campers)
                shimmying
down to Sweetgrass   heat waves
        (off tarred blacktop)
lie liquid
somewhere ahead over an invisible
                    border
like sweet Sunday beer

backed into a trestle
my flesh formed by one
girder in a Canadian
Pacific grid   facing South
upstream   I am dazed
by the sun   sights
mirages

                    I see

a land of: Sunday boundaries

between beer and no beer

              :   bridges

over the only gaps in the flatness

              :   monuments

(old and new) constructed by/for trespassers

              :   peace

when the West wind blows

and everything leans with it

diplomatically

(iii) KILLING FLOOR RESOLUTIONS

a knife has driven
softly in from the East
and beef cows
                slow   slow animals
have fallen in the strange breeze
I smell them
hear their blood guts spilling
fatly   splatting
beef cows die with an easy heave
numbered days of fatting grains
        nights of fluorescent eating
ending

buffalo
refusing corrals and fences
and selective breeding
thundered over blind cliffs
died

young and peacefully

only fat and complacent

nationless

immigrants

remain

Charolais and Angus and Simental

they have no allegiance

but to their select grains

and the owners who supply it

as long as it is profitable

these cows deserve their dining-table fate

and the wind carries their death to me

as I attempt to define directions

seek a new boundary

a new North

that denies intrusions

        domineering West winds

        thirsty Southern suns

        even soft insidious approaches

from the East

I will leave at night

when the air is calm and cold and quiet

I will listen for the buffalo

who have gone before

to warn of bluffs

I will go North

Lorne Daniel was born in 1953 and grew up in west-central Alberta. He now lives and works in Edmonton. He was included by Al Purdy in *STORM WARNING 2*. *TOWARDS A NEW COMPASS* is his second book of poems.

THISTLEDOWN BOOKS

WIND SONGS by Glen Sorestad

DARK HONEY by Ronald Marken

INSIDE IS THE SKY by Lorna Uher

OCTOMI by Andrew Suknaski

SUMMER'S BRIGHT BLOOD by William Latta

PRAIRIE PUB POEMS by Glen Sorestad

PORTRAITS by Lala Koehn

HAIL STORM by Peter Christensen

BETWEEN THE LINES by Stephen Scriver

GATHERING FIRE by Helen Hawley

TOWARDS A NEW COMPASS by Lorne Daniel